Self Portrait, 1927

VICTORIA AND ALBERT MUSEUM

The Engraved Work of
ERIC GILL

London: Her Majesty's Stationery Office 1963

Large Picture Book No. 17

© *Crown copyright 1963*

Printed in England for Her Majesty's Stationery Office
by The Curwen Press Ltd., Plaistow, London, E.13

In 1952 Mrs. Gill, widow of Eric Gill, generously gave to the Victoria and Albert Museum her husband's file copies of his engravings; this valuable gift comprised virtually the whole of his work as an engraver on wood and metal. The present Picture Book contains a representative selection of his varied achievement in this field, depicting both religious and secular subjects, and ranging in date from 1908 until the artist's death in 1940. It is published in conjunction with a Catalogue of the engravings compiled by Mr. John Physick. of the Department of Prints and Drawings.

1963   TRENCHARD COX
                                                Director

INTRODUCTION

THIS Picture Book contains reproductions of 206 engravings on wood and metal by Eric Gill, chosen almost entirely from the comprehensive collection given to the Department of Prints and Drawings by his widow in 1952. It is designed to give a representative survey over the whole of his working career from 1908 to 1940. While complete in itself, it is issued in conjunction with the Catalogue of Mrs. Gill's gift published by H.M.S.O., price 27s. 6d., which gives full bibliographical details of the entire collection.

Arthur Eric Rowton Gill, sculptor, engraver, typographer and writer, was born at Brighton in 1882, the son of a Minister of the Countess of Huntingdon's Connection who later became an Anglican. He was at first a student at Chichester Art School, and then between 1900 and 1903 was articled to the architect W. D. Caroë in London. During this period he became interested in lettering and went to the Central School of Arts and Crafts, where he studied under Edward Johnston, and with whom he eventually shared rooms in Lincoln's Inn.

From 1903 Gill was able to earn his living as a letter-cutter, and in 1904 he married Mary Ethel Moore. After living for a short time in Battersea and Hammersmith, Gill and his wife settled at Ditchling, Sussex in 1907. A few years later Edward Johnston and Hilary Pepler also went to Ditchling, where by 1915 Pepler had started his St. Dominic's Press. During the next nine years Gill made over 200 engravings, many of which were used several times by Pepler in his publications. Of these mention might be made of the occasional magazine *The Game* (Plates 16, 22, 23, 35, 37, 50, 59, 68); *The Way of the Cross*, 1917 (Plates 22, 33); the *Horae Beatae Virginis Mariae . . .*, 1923 (Plates 29, 30, 31, 32, 45, 50); and the series of 'Welfare Handbooks' (Plates 16, 26, 35, 36, 51, 71), some of which were written by Gill himself.

He was converted to Roman Catholicism in 1913, and in the following year was commissioned to carve the Stations of the Cross in Westminster Cathedral, a task which occupied him for four years, until 1918. After a short spell in the army at the end of the First World War, Gill returned to Ditchling where he and others formed the Guild of St. Joseph and St. Dominic, a semi-religious community of craftsmen, and it was about this time that he became a Tertiary of the Order of St. Dominic.

In 1924 he and his family moved to Capel-y-ffin in the Black Mountains of Wales near Abergavenny, where they lived in a former monastery belonging to the Benedictine Abbey of Caldey Island. It was at Capel-y-ffin that Gill began his connection with the Golden Cockerel Press of Robert Gibbings and continued his work for the Cranach Press of Count Kessler in Weimar. Also at this period Stanley Morison asked him to design lettering for the Monotype Corporation, which resulted in the creation of the 'Perpetua' and 'Sans-serif' printing types. (This Picture Book is printed in 'Perpetua' and the Catalogue in 'Sans-serif'.) Among the books illustrated by Gill at this time were the Golden Cockerel Press *Troilus and Criseyde* (Plates 122–128, 130), *Procreant Hymn* by

E. Powys Mathers (Plates 105, 118), *The Song of Songs* (Plates 110, 119), *Passio Domini Nostri Jesu Christi* (Plate 98), and *Id Quod Visum Placet* (Plates 100, 107), the latter being written by himself.

Gill and his family eventually found that living at Capel-y-ffin was no longer convenient, and in 1928 they moved to Pigotts at Speen, near High Wycombe in Buckinghamshire. Here Gill engraved for *The Canterbury Tales* (Plates 134, 135, 143, 158–163) and *The Four Gospels* (Plates 141, 145, 164–166) of the Golden Cockerel Press, *Canticum Canticorum* (Plates 146, 147, 148, 152–155) of the Cranach Press, and *Hamlet* (Plates 170, 183) and *Henry the Eighth* (Plate 189), which were published by the Limited Editions Club, New York. He continued to design printing types, worked on the sculpture for Broadcasting House, London, and the League of Nations Building, Geneva, and also went to Jerusalem to carve panels for the new Museum there. He and his son-in-law René Hague established their own printing press at Pigotts, on which much of his later work was printed, such as *Engravings 1928–1933*, *The Passion of Our Lord* (Plates 174, 175), *Twenty-five nudes* (Plate 190), and *The Holy Sonnets of John Donne* (Plate 200). Gill was appointed R.D.I. in 1936 and A.R.A. in 1937. He died at Harefield, Middlesex, in November 1940 and is buried in the churchyard at Speen.

Eric Gill was a deeply religious man, and to him art was 'man's act of collaboration with God in creating'. In *Drawings from Life*, 1940, he writes 'that it seems best to draw whatever is natural and normal and trust to the good sense of people to see things in a reasonable manner': his interpretation of the natural and normal, however, still causes some of his work to be labelled indecent or erotic. He held strong views against machines and machine-made things, and his disapproval of the social and economic trends of his time are reflected in his engravings and writings.

Besides his hundreds of engravings for book illustration Gill engraved many detached plates and ephemera: book-plates (Plates 5, 55, 66, 67, 77, 102, 103, 114, 140, 171, 179, 185, 191), Christmas cards (Plates 2, 20, 45, 56, 204), portraits (Frontispiece, Plates 3, 64, 79, 80), and Ordination cards (Plates 113, 201). In all he produced just over 1000 engravings on wood and metal, and in 1952 his widow, Mrs. Mary Gill, gave to the Department of Prints and Drawings her husband's personal file copies which constituted an almost complete record of his work. In the same year Mr. Douglas Cleverdon, who in 1929 had published the first catalogue of the engravings, gave a number of those prints which were not included in Mrs. Gill's gift. Consequently the Victoria and Albert Museum possesses what is probably the most comprehensive collection of Eric Gill's work in existence, and this Picture Book illustrates nearly a quarter of this rich mass of material.

J.P.

LIST OF PLATES

The majority of the engravings have been reproduced in their actual size. However, some which were too large to permit of this have been slightly reduced. The descriptions of the plates give the titles used by the artist and include the sizes in inches, height before width in all cases. The number in brackets following the description of each item (e.g. J.P. 4) refers to the entry in the companion volume to this Picture Book, the *Catalogue of the Engraved Work of Eric Gill* by J. F. Physick, H.M.S.O., 1963.

Cover design. The Lion of St. Mark (see No. 165).

Frontispiece. Self Portrait. 1927. (J.P. 497, final state)
Wood-engraving. $7 \times 4\frac{7}{8}$ E.1324–1952

1. Chalice and Host with particles. Design for Messrs. Burns & Oates Ltd., London. 1914. (J.P. 19, 2nd state)
Wood-engraving. $2\frac{3}{8} \times 1\frac{1}{2}$ E.831–1952

2. Christmas Card of the artist and his wife. 1908. (J.P. 8)
Wood-engraving. $1\frac{3}{8} \times 3$ E.818–1952

3. Self Portrait. Design used on a postcard by the artist. 1908. (J.P. 4)
Wood-engraving. $1\frac{1}{8} \times \frac{7}{8}$ E.2122–1952

4. Hand and eye. 1908. Subsequently used as a printer's device by Francis Walterson, Capel-y-ffin, Abergavenny, 1928. (J.P. 7)
Woodcut. $1\frac{3}{8} \times 1$ E.817–1952

5. Book-plate of Isabella Hildebrand. 1909. (J.P. 9)
Wood-engraving. $1\frac{1}{4} \times 2\frac{3}{8}$ E.819–1952

6. Design for a card commemorating Henry Holding Moore, father of the artist's wife. 1911. (J.P. 12)
Wood-engraving. $2\frac{1}{2} \times 2\frac{1}{2}$ E.822–1952

7. The Slaughter of the Innocents. Design for the cover of the catalogue of an exhibition in aid of Belgian refugees. 1914. (J.P. 18)
Wood-engraving. $2\frac{3}{8} \times 2$ E.828–1952

8. Crucifix. 1913. (J.P. 16, 3rd state)
Wood-engraving. $7\frac{1}{8} \times 2\frac{3}{4}$ E.827–1952

9. Child and Ghost. Illustration on page 3 of *Concerning Dragons*, a rhyme by H. D. C. Pepler, No. 9 of the publications of St. Dominic's Press. 1916. (J.P. 69)
Wood-engraving. $1\frac{1}{2} \times 1\frac{1}{2}$ E.900–1952

10. Decoy Duck. Imprint for the Decoy Press. 1915. (J.P. 35, ? final state)
Wood-engraving. $2\frac{3}{8} \times 1\frac{5}{8}$ E.848–1952

11. Chalice and Host. Illustration on the front cover of *Serving at Mass*, compiled by the artist, No. 10 of the publications of St. Dominic's Press. 1916. (J.P. 65, 2nd state)
Woodcut. $1\frac{1}{2} \times 3\frac{1}{4}$ E.995(2)–1952

12. St. Michael and the Dragon. Illustration on the title-page to *Concerning Dragons*, a rhyme by H. D. C. Pepler, No. 9 of the publications of St. Dominic's Press. 1916. (J.P. 66)
Wood-engraving. $2\frac{3}{4} \times 2\frac{1}{8}$ E.897–1952

13. Invitation. Illustration on page 7 of *Three Poems* by Ananda K. Coomaraswamy, printed by St. Dominic's Press, for private distribution. 1920. (J.P. 164)
Woodcut. $1\frac{3}{4} \times 1\frac{3}{8}$ E.988–1952

14. Flight into Egypt. 1916. (J.P. 52)
Wood-engraving. $2\frac{3}{8} \times 2$ E.878–1952

15. Woman. An experiment in blind printing. 1914. (J.P. 24)
Woodcut. $6 \times 3\frac{1}{8}$ E.838–1952

16. Gravestone with Angel. Design for the cover of *An Elegy upon Old Freeman* by Matthew Stevenson, published by Everard Meynell, London. 1916. (J.P. 61, early state)
Wood-engraving. $1\frac{1}{8} \times 1\frac{1}{4}$ E.891–1952

17. Hog and Wheatsheaf. Design for printing on paper bags for the Hampshire House Bakery, Doves Lane, Hammersmith. 1915. (J.P. 31)
Wood-engraving. Circular, diameter 5⅜ E.844–1952

18. The Taking of Toll. Frontispiece to *The Taking of Toll being the Danā Lilā of Rājendra*, translated by Ananda K. Coomaraswamy, published by the Old Bourne Press, London. 1915. (J.P. 33)
Woodcut. 5¼ × 4 E.846–1952

19. Animals All. 1916. (J.P. 50)
Wood-engraving. 2¼ × 2¼ E.876–1952

20. Madonna and Child: Madonna kneeling. Design for a Christmas Card. 1914. (J.P. 30, 1st state)
Wood-engraving. 2⅜ × 2¼ E.872–1952

21. The Happy Labourer. Illustration on page 82 of *The Devil's Devices* by H. D. C. Pepler, published by the Hampshire House Workshops, London. 1915. (J.P. 42, 4th state)
Wood-engraving. 5⅜ × 3⅜ E.861–1952

22. D P and Cross. Design for St. Dominic's Press, Ditchling, Sussex. 1916. (J.P. 64)
Woodcut. 1¼ × ⅜ E.895–1952

23. Circular device. Illustration on page 31, Volume I, Number 2 of *The Game*, published by St. Dominic's Press, December 1916. (J.P. 78)
Wood-engraving. Circular, diameter 1⅝ E.907–1952

24. Lettering with nib: a b c x c, for a copy sheet illustrating handwriting by Edward Johnston, published by H. D. C. Pepler at Hampshire House, Hammersmith. 1916. (J.P. 71)
Woodcut. 1 × 1⅝ E.963–1952

25. Hottentot. 1920. (J.P. 172, early state)
Woodcut. 8 × 2 E.997–1952

26. The Last Judgment. Illustration to a broadsheet published by St. Dominic's Press. 1917. (J.P. 107)
Wood-engraving. 1⅞ × 2¼ E.939–1952

27. Diagram for Ice-House. Illustration on page 165 of Cobbett's *Cottage Economy*, with an introduction by G. K. Chesterton, published by the Hampshire House Workshops, London. 1916. (J.P. 57)
Wood-engraving. 5¼ × 2¾ E.886–1952

28. Adam and Eve. Illustration on page 40 of *God and the Dragon*, rhymes by H. D. C. Pepler, No. 15 of the publications of St. Dominic's Press. 1917. (J.P. 87)
Woodcut. 1¾ × 2⅜ E.915–1952

29. Madonna and Child with Chalice. Illustration on the title-page to *Adeste Fideles a Christmas Hymn*, No. 12 of the publications of St. Dominic's Press. 1916. (J.P. 76)
Wood-engraving. 2½ × 1¾ E.905–1952

30. Epiphany. Illustration on page 1 of *God and the Dragon*. 1917. (J.P. 84)
Wood-engraving. 1¾ × 2½ E.912–1952

31. Parlers. Illustration on page 27 of *God and the Dragon*. 1917. (J.P. 85, 2nd state)
Wood-engraving. 1⅝ × 2¼ E.913(2)–1952

32. Palm Sunday. Illustration on page 6 of *God and the Dragon*. 1917. (J.P. 86)
Wood-engraving. 1⅝ × 2½ E.914–1952

33. Jesus dies upon the Cross. Illustration of Station XII, after the artist's Stations of the Cross in Westminster Cathedral, on page 20 of *The Way of the Cross*, No. 17 of the publications of St. Dominic's Press. 1917. (J.P. 104, final state)
Wood-engraving. 2⅜ × 2⅜ E.936–1952

34. Spray of leaves. Design to illustrate a funeral card, printed by St. Dominic's Press. 1917. (J.P. 108, final state)
Wood-engraving. 1⅛ × 1½ E.941–1952

35. Paschal Lamb. Illustration on page 40, Volume I, Number 3 of *The Game*, published by St. Dominic's Press, Easter 1917. (J.P. 92, final state)
Wood-engraving. Circular, diameter 1⅞ E.922–1952

36. Initial letter O with speedwell. Design to illustrate a funeral card, printed by St. Dominic's Press. 1917. (J.P. 110)
Wood-engraving. 1⅛ × 1⅛ E.943–1952

37. Welsh Dragon. Illustration on page 13, Volume III, Number 1 of *The Game*, published by St. Dominic's Press, Corpus Christi 1919. (J.P. 150)
Wood-engraving. ⅞ × 1⅛ E.971–1952

38. Flower. Design for Ethel Mairet of Ditchling. 1918. (J.P. 139)
Wood-engraving. Circular, diameter ⅝ E.962–1952

39. Crucifix: En Ego. Illustration on page 14 of *Nisi Dominus*, rimes by H. D. C. Pepler, No. 29 of the publications of St. Dominic's Press, 1919. 1918. (J.P. 148)
Wood-engraving. 1⅞ × 1½ E.980–1952

40. Penny Pie. Tail-piece on page 5 of *Three Poems* by H. D. C. Pepler, published by St. Dominic's Press. 1918. (J.P. 144)
Wood-engraving. $\frac{5}{8} \times \frac{5}{8}$ E.970–1952

41. Hand and Cross. 1920. The design was used as a letter-heading by H. D. C. Pepler. (J.P. 161)
Wood-engraving. $\frac{5}{8} \times \frac{3}{8}$ E.985–1952

42. Tail-piece on page 37 of *Wood-engraving* by R. John Beedham, No. 10 of the publications of St. Dominic's Press. 1920. (J.P. 169)
Wood-engraving. $\frac{7}{8} \times 1\frac{3}{8}$ E.993–1952

43. Dominican Shield. 1918. (J.P. 149a)
Woodcut. $1\frac{1}{4} \times 1$ E.982–1952

44. Stalk with leaves. Design to illustrate a funeral card printed by St. Dominic's Press. 1917. (J.P. 109)
Wood-engraving. 1×1 E.942–1952

45. Madonna and Child in vesica. Christmas Card. 1918. (J.P. 143)
Wood-engraving. $4\frac{1}{4} \times 1\frac{3}{4}$ E.969–1952

46. Handscrew; G cramp; plane. Illustrations on page 17 of *Woodwork* by A. Romney Green, No. 26 of the publications of St. Dominic's Press, 1918. 1917. (J.P. 123, 124, 124a)
Wood-engravings. Overall size 2×3 E.952–1952
Note: *The engraving of the plane was not used in the book, nor was it given a serial number by the artist in his records.*

47. View of Ditchling. Design for the Ditchling Women's Institute. 1918. (J.P. 138, 1st state)
Wood-engraving. $\frac{7}{8} \times 2\frac{3}{8}$ E.960–1952

48. Three Martlets [*sic*]. Design for Messrs. Burns & Oates Ltd., London. 1914. (J.P. 28)
Wood-engraving. $2\frac{5}{8} \times 2\frac{1}{8}$ E.842–1952
Note: *In this design which represents the coat of arms of Thomas à Becket, the birds depicted are Cornish choughs and were erroneously described by the artist as martlets.*

49. The Holy Face. 1917. (J.P. 111, early state)
Wood-engraving. $3\frac{1}{8} \times 2\frac{1}{4}$ E.944–1952

50. The Resurrection. Illustration on page 37, Volume I, Number 3 of *The Game*, published by St. Dominic's Press, Easter 1917. (J.P. 91, 1st state)
Wood-engraving. $5\frac{5}{8} \times 3\frac{5}{8}$ E.919–1952

51. Christ and the Money-Changers. Illustration on page iii of *Riches*, Welfare Handbook No. 3, No. 28(3) of the publications of St. Dominic's Press. 1919. (J.P. 152)
Wood-engraving. $2\frac{1}{8} \times 3\frac{1}{8}$ E.973–1952

52. Spoil Bank Crucifix, with chapel [Ditchling, Sussex]. 1919. (J.P. 156)
Wood-engraving. $2\frac{7}{8} \times 4$ E.978–1952

53. New England Woods. Illustration on page 2 of *Three Poems* by Ananda K. Coomaraswamy, printed by St. Dominic's Press, for private distribution. 1920. (J.P. 163)
Woodcut. $3\frac{3}{4} \times 2\frac{3}{8}$ E.987–1952

54. Penguin. 1920. (J.P. 170)
Woodcut. $3\frac{1}{4} \times 2\frac{1}{8}$ E.994–1952

55. Girl with deer. Book-plate of Ananda K. Coomaraswamy. 1920. (J.P. 173)
Wood-engraving. $2\frac{1}{2} \times 2\frac{1}{2}$ E.998–1952

56. Bambino. Design for a Christmas Card. 1910. (J.P. 174)
Woodcut. $2\frac{1}{8} \times 1\frac{3}{4}$ E.999–1952

57. Lawyer's Wig. Illustration on the cover-title to *The Law the Lawyers Know About*, No. 9(a) of the publications of St. Dominic's Press. 1923. (J.P. 230)
Wood-engraving. $1 \times \frac{5}{8}$ E.1064–1952

58. St. Martin. Design for the letter-heading of R. F. Martin. 1922. (J.P. 212, 2nd state)
Wood-engraving. $1\frac{1}{2} \times 1\frac{1}{4}$ E.1091(2)–1952

59. The Blessed Trinity with the Blessed Virgin. Illustration, after a drawing by Elizabeth Gill, on page 17, Volume IV, Number 2 of *The Game*, published by St. Dominic's Press, February 1921. (J.P. 181)
Wood-engraving. $3\frac{1}{8} \times 3\frac{3}{4}$ E.1006–1952

60. Tree and Burin. Design for the Society of Wood-Engravers, used as an illustration on the front covers of the catalogues of their annual exhibitions. (J.P. 188, early state)
Lettered W-E.
Wood-engraving. $2\frac{1}{8} \times 1\frac{3}{4}$ E.1015–1952
Note: *The final state of this engraving is without the letters 'W-E' and is signed in reverse 'EG'.*

61. The Lion. 1921. (J.P. 179, final state)
Wood-engraving. $2\frac{1}{4} \times 3\frac{1}{8}$ E.1004–1952
Note: *This design is also known as 'She loves me not'.*

62. Nude Crucifix. The block was subsequently carved. 1922. (J.P. 192, late state)
Lettered INRI.
Wood-engraving. $4\frac{1}{2} \times 1\frac{1}{2}$ E.1019–1952

63. Westward Ho! Engraved after a drawing by David Jones. 1921. (J.P. 185)
Wood-engraving. $5 \times 3\frac{5}{8}$ E.1010–1952

64. Clare [portrait of Mrs. H. D. C. Pepler]. 1922. (J.P. 196, early state)
Wood-engraving. $6\frac{5}{8} \times 4\frac{5}{8}$ E.1023–1952

65. The Thorn in the Flesh. 1921. (J.P. 184)
Wood-engraving. $4\frac{7}{8} \times 4\frac{1}{8}$ E.1009–1952

66. Madonna and Child. Book-plate of the Rev. Desmond Chute. 1923. (J.P. 216)
Wood-engraving. $2\frac{3}{4} \times 1\frac{1}{4}$ E.1050–1952

67. St. Martin. Book-plate, after a design by David Jones, of Thomas Lowinsky. 1922. (J.P. 207)
Wood-engraving. $3\frac{3}{4} \times 2\frac{3}{4}$ E.1038–1952

68. Nuptials of God. Illustration on page 3, Volume VI, Number 34 of *The Game*, published by St. Dominic's Press, January 1923. 1922. (J.P. 214)
Wood-engraving. $2\frac{5}{8} \times 2$ E.1048–1952

69. St. George and the Dragon. Design for the Lancashire Catholic Players. 1922. (J.P. 213)
Wood-engraving. $1\frac{1}{2} \times 1\frac{7}{8}$ E.1047–1952

70. St. Sebastian. The block was subsequently carved. 1922. (J.P. 200)
Wood-engraving. $4\frac{1}{4} \times 1\frac{1}{2}$ E.2128–1952

71. Dress, 1920. Illustration on page 1 of *Dress*, Welfare Handbook No. 7, by the artist, No. 28(7) of the publications of St. Dominic's Press. Engraved after a drawing by Edward Sullivan for *A Modern Utopia* by H. G. Wells. (J.P. 186)
Wood-engraving. $3\frac{3}{4} \times 3\frac{1}{8}$ E.1011–1925

72. Clock Tower [Ingatestone, Essex]. 1922. (J.P. 203)
Woodcut. $2\frac{1}{4} \times 2\frac{1}{8}$ E.1033–1952

73. Mary at the Sepulchre. Engraved after a drawing by David Jones and subsequently carved. 1923. (J.P. 262)
Wood-engraving. $3 \times 2\frac{1}{4}$ E.1096–1952

74. Autumn Midnight. Frontispiece to *Autumn Midnight* by Frances Cornford, printed by St. Dominic's Press, published by The Poetry Book-shop, London. 1923. (J.P. 231)
Wood-engraving. $4\frac{5}{8} \times 3\frac{1}{4}$ E.1065–1952

75. Girl in Bath, II [portrait of Petra, the artist's daughter). (J.P. 218)
Wood-engraving. $4\frac{1}{4} \times 4\frac{1}{8}$ E.1052–1952

76. Daily Herald Order of Industrial Heroism. 1923.
Wood-engravings and letterpress. Size of sheet $7\frac{3}{4} \times 9\frac{1}{2}$
    E.1055–1952

    St. Christopher. (J.P. 220) $5 \times 2\frac{1}{2}$
    A rose-plant in Jericho. (J.P. 221) $4\frac{3}{4} \times 2\frac{5}{8}$
    Wave. (J.P. 222) $\frac{1}{2} \times 2\frac{3}{4}$
    Five-pointed star. (J.P. 223) $1\frac{1}{8} \times 1$

77. Jesuit Martyr. Book-plate of James Comly McCoy. 1923. (J.P. 263, final state)
Wood-engraving. $3\frac{1}{2} \times 2\frac{3}{8}$ E.1099–1952

78. Mother and Child. Illustration on page 24 of *Sonnets and Verses* by Enid Clay, No. 25 of the publications of the Golden Cockerel Press, Waltham St. Lawrence, Berkshire, 1925. 1924. (J.P. 286)
Wood-engraving. $3\frac{3}{8} \times 3\frac{3}{8}$ E.1124–1952

79. Gordian Gill. 1924. (J.P. 280)
Engraving. $8\frac{1}{8} \times 6$ E.1116–1952

80. Teresa and Winifred Maxwell. 1923. (J.P. 255, early state)
Wood-engraving. $4\frac{1}{8} \times 4\frac{5}{8}$ E.1089–1952
Note: *This state is without the engraved names of the sitters.*

81. Naked Girl lying on Grass. Illustration on page 17 of *Sonnets and Verses* by Enid Clay, 1925. 1924. (J.P. 284)
Wood-engraving $1\frac{5}{8} \times 3\frac{1}{8}$ E.1122–1952

82. Flower-piece. Illustration on page 32 of *Sonnets and Verses* by Enid Clay, 1925. 1924. (J.P. 281)
Wood-engraving. $5\frac{1}{4} \times 3\frac{7}{8}$ E.1117–1952

83. Death and the Lady. Illustration on page 10 of *Sonnets and Verses* by Enid Clay, 1925. 1924. (J.P. 285)
Wood-engraving. $5\frac{1}{8} \times 3\frac{3}{8}$ E.1123–1952

84–88. Initial letters for *Autumn Midnight* by Frances Cornford. 1923.

    84. W with woman and child, on page 8. (J.P. 237)
    Wood-engraving. $\frac{7}{8} \times 1\frac{3}{4}$ E.1070–1952
    85. T with man and thistles, on page 7. (J.P. 236)
    Wood-engraving. $\frac{7}{8} \times \frac{7}{8}$ E.1069–1952

86. A with princess and gipsy, on page 12. (J.P. 242)
Wood-engraving. $1 \times 1\frac{1}{8}$ E.1075–1952

87. C with bird-cage, on page 18. (J.P. 245)
Wood-engraving. $\frac{7}{8} \times \frac{3}{4}$ E.1078–1952

88. A with woman and child, on page 7. (J.P. 235)
Wood-engraving. $1\frac{1}{8} \times 1$ E.1068–1952

89. Woman's Head. Experiment in cross-hatching. 1923. (J.P. 229)
Wood-engraving. $1\frac{5}{8} \times 1\frac{1}{2}$ E.1063–1952

90. Figure of a girl, seated. 1923. The block was subsequently carved. (J.P. 267)
Wood-engraving. $1\frac{3}{8} \times 1\frac{1}{2}$ E.1102–1952

91. Crown of Thorns. Illustration to 'St. Thomas Aquinas Calendar 1925', published by St. Dominic's Press, 1924. 1923. (J.P. 252)
Wood-engraving. $\frac{3}{4} \times \frac{3}{4}$ E.1085–1952

92. Sacred Heart with Crown of Thorns. Illustration to 'St. Thomas Aquinas Calendar 1925', published by St. Dominic's Press, 1924. 1923. (J.P. 251)
Wood-engraving. $\frac{3}{4} \times \frac{3}{4}$ E.1084–1952

93. The Bee Sting. 1924. (J.P. 292, 2nd state)
Wood-engraving. $5\frac{1}{8} \times 2$ E.1135–1952

94. Venus. 1924. (J.P. 290, 2nd state)
Wood-engraving. $5\frac{3}{8} \times 1\frac{1}{2}$ E.1130–1952

95. Youth and Love. Illustration on the title-page to *Sonnets and Verses* by Enid Clay, 1925. 1924. (J.P. 283)
Wood-engraving. $1\frac{3}{4} \times 2\frac{3}{4}$ E.1121–1952

96. The Holy Ghost as Dove. Design originally incorporated in the 'Daily Herald Order of Industrial Heroism'. 1923. (J.P. 224)
Wood-engraving. $1\frac{3}{8} \times 1\frac{1}{2}$ E.1056–1952

97. Safety First. 1924. (J.P. 295)
Wood-engraving. $6 \times 6\frac{1}{2}$ E.1139–1952

98. The Crucifixion. Illustration on page 12 of *Passio Domini Nostri Jesu Christi*, No. 35 of the publications of the Golden Cockerel Press. 1926. (J.P. 353)
Wood-engraving. $6\frac{1}{8} \times 4\frac{1}{8}$ E.1203–1952

99. Adam and Eve in Heaven, or the Public-House in Paradise. Illustration to face page 1 of *Art & Love* by the artist, printed by the Golden Cockerel Press for Douglas Cleverdon, Bristol, 1928. 1927. (J.P. 480)
Engraving. $4\frac{1}{2} \times 2\frac{3}{4}$ E.1305–1952

100. Flying Buttresses [St. Pierre, Chartres]. Illustration to face page 10 of *Id Quod Visum Placet* by the artist, printed by the Golden Cockerel Press for the author, Capel-y-ffin, Abergavenny. 1926. (J.P. 373)
Engraving. $4\frac{1}{2} \times 2\frac{3}{4}$ E.1221–1952

101. The Shepherds. 1924. (J.P. 301)
Wood-engraving, intaglio print. $2\frac{7}{8} \times 3\frac{1}{4}$
     E.1145–1952

102. Book-plate of the Hon. Ralph Edward Gathorne-Hardy. 1925. (J.P. 307)
Engraving. $4 \times 2\frac{1}{2}$ E.1151–1952

103. Girl with Three Scallops. Book-plate of Kate Fletcher. 1927. (J.P. 492)
Engraving. $3\frac{1}{2} \times 2\frac{1}{4}$ E.1318–1952

104. Roundel, with a crouching figure by Aristide Maillol, and lettering by Eric Gill. Device in *P. Vergilii Maronis Eclogae & Georgica Latine Et Germanice Volumen Primus: Eclogae*, revised by Thomas Achelis and Alfred Körte, printed by the Cranach Press and published by Insel-Verlag, Leipzig, 1926. 1925. (J.P. 313)
Woodcut. Circular, diameter $2\frac{1}{2}$ E.1158–1952

105. Earth Waiting. Illustration to face page 8 of *Procreant Hymn* by E. Powys Mathers, No. 37 of the publications of the Golden Cockerel Press, 1926. (J.P. 360)
Engraving. $4\frac{1}{2} \times 3\frac{1}{2}$ E.1208–1952

106. Crucifix. 1926. (J.P. 376)
Engraving. 7×5 E.1224–1952

107. St. Thomas's Hands. Design for the title-page to *Id Quod Visum Placet* by the artist. 1926. (J.P. 382)
Wood-engraving. $1\frac{3}{8} \times 1\frac{5}{8}$ E.1229–1952

108. Boy with drawing-board. Design for the title-page to *The Architects' Journal*, published by The Architectural Press, London, first used 6 January 1926. 1925. (J.P. 346)
Wood-engraving. $1\frac{1}{2} \times 1\frac{7}{8}$ E.1197–1952

109. St. Bernadette. 1926. (J.P. 381)
Wood-engraving. $4\frac{1}{4} \times 3\frac{1}{4}$ E.1228–1952

110. A Garden enclosed. Illustration on page 27 of *The Song of Songs*. 1925. (J.P. 324)
Wood-engraving. $2 \times 1\frac{3}{4}$ E.1172–1952

111. Child with letter T as Crucifix. Tail-piece on page 310 of Chaucer's *Troilus and Criseyde*. 1927. (J.P. 487)
Wood-engraving. $1\frac{3}{4} \times 1\frac{3}{4}$ E.1312–1952

112. Eve. 1926. (J.P. 380)
Wood-engraving. $9\frac{1}{2} \times 4\frac{3}{4}$ E.1227–1952

113. The Good Shepherd. Design for the Ordination Card of the Rev. Desmond Chute. 1927. (J.P. 489)
Wood-engraving. $3\frac{3}{8} \times 1\frac{7}{8}$ E.1315–1952

114. A Snake. Book-plate designed for the Rev. John Gray for Mark André Raffalovich. 1925. (J.P. 335)
Wood-engraving. $\frac{1}{2} \times 2\frac{3}{8}$ E.1183–1952

115. The Convert. 1925. (J.P. 308)
Wood-engraving. $3\frac{5}{8} \times 2\frac{5}{8}$ E.1152–1952

116. Girl in leaves. Design for a tail-piece. 1926. (J.P. 386)
Wood-engraving. $1\frac{1}{4} \times 2$ E.1231(2)–1952

117. Woman bending. 1926. (J.P. 388, 2nd state)
Wood-engraving. $2\frac{1}{2} \times 2$ E.1233–1952

118. Dalliance. Illustration to face page 15 of *Procreant Hymn* by E. Powys Mathers. 1926. (J.P. 362)
Engraving. $4\frac{1}{2} \times 3\frac{1}{2}$ E.1210–1952

119. On my Bed by Night. Illustration on page 20 of *The Song of Songs*, No. 31 of the publications of the Golden Cockerel Press. 1925. (J.P. 320)
Wood-engraving. $2\frac{5}{8} \times 3\frac{7}{8}$ E.1168–1952

120. The Bird in the Bush. Illustration to face page 1 of *Art & Prudence* by the artist, No. 61 of the publications of the Golden Cockerel Press. 1928. (J.P. 505)
Engraving. $4\frac{5}{8} \times 3$ E.1331–1952

121. The Skaters. After a photograph in the *Daily Mirror*. 1926. (J.P. 368, 2nd state)
Engraving. $4\frac{1}{2} \times 4\frac{1}{2}$ E.1216–1952

122–127. Decorative borders to Chaucer's *Troilus and Criseyde*, No. 50 of the publications of the Golden Cockerel Press, 1927.

122. Naked Youth. Border on pages 28, 56, 92, 122, 150 and 280. (J.P. 423)
Wood-engraving. $7 \times 1\frac{1}{4}$ E.1259(1)–1952

123. Naked Girl looking back. Border on pages 29, 49, 123, 151, 192 and 281. (J.P. 424)
Wood-engraving. $7 \times 1\frac{3}{4}$ E.1259(2)–1952

124. Man with Raised Sword. Border on pages 24, 52, 188, 210, 228, 264 and 298. (J.P. 439)
Wood-engraving. $7 \times 1\frac{1}{4}$ E.1271(1)–1952

125. Cupid running, Ape and Satyr in Tree. Border on pages 3, 25, 111, 197, 229, 265 and 291. (J.P. 440)
Wood-engraving. $7 \times 1\frac{1}{2}$ E.1271(2)–1952

126. Chaucer and Cupid. Border on pages 2, 106, 176 and 234. (J.P. 443)
Wood-engraving. $6\frac{7}{8} \times 1\frac{1}{4}$ E.1273(1)–1952

127. Chaucer writing. Border on page 179. (J.P. 444)
Wood-engraving. $7 \times 1\frac{3}{4}$ E.1273(2)–1952

128. Initial letters for use in Chaucer's *Troilus and Criseyde*. 1927. (J.P. 477)
Woodcuts. Various sizes E.1300–1952

129. An alphabet. Letters designed for the Golden Cockerel Press. 1928. (J.P. 552)
Woodcuts. Various sizes E.1357–1952

130. Approaching Dawn. Illustration on page 12 of Chaucer's *Troilus and Criseyde*. 1927. (J.P. 470)
Wood-engraving. $7 \times 4\frac{1}{2}$ E.1291–1952

131. Nativity. Illustration on page 1 of *Gloria in Profundis* by G. K. Chesterton, published by Faber & Gwyer Ltd., London. 1927. (J.P. 479, 1st state)
Wood-engraving. $4\frac{7}{8} \times 3\frac{1}{8}$ E.1302–1952

132. Marbling. Illustration on page 249, Volume I of *Tristram Shandy* by Laurence Sterne, No. 66 of the publications of the Golden Cockerel Press. 1929. (J.P. 561)
Wood-engraving. $5\frac{3}{4} \times 3\frac{3}{4}$ E.1368–1952

133. Leda loved. Frontispiece to *Leda* by Aldous Huxley. 1929. (J.P. 617, final state)
Wood-engraving. $5\frac{3}{8} \times 3\frac{1}{4}$ E.1407–1952

134. Initial letter H, and Venus and Cupid with the Golden Cockerel. Illustration on page 1, Volume I of Chaucer's *The Canterbury Tales*. 1928. (J.P. 535)
Wood-engraving. $6\frac{1}{2} \times 5\frac{1}{8}$ E.1347(1)–1952

135. The Parson's Tale. Initial letter O and an illustration on page 123, Volume IV of Chaucer's *The Canterbury Tales*, 1931. 1920. (J.P. 677)
Wood-engraving. $6\frac{3}{4} \times 5\frac{1}{4}$ E.1456–1952

136. Amnon. Frontispiece to *The Story of Amnon*, No. 1 of the publications of René Hague and Eric Gill at Pigotts. 1930. (J.P. 709)
Wood-engraving. $3\frac{1}{8} \times 2\frac{5}{8}$ E.1479–1952

137. Girl sitting in leaves: Belle Sauvage I. Illustration on page 205 of *The Legion Book*, edited by Captain H. Cotton Minchin, published by The Curwen Press, London. 1929. (J.P. 558)
Wood-engraving. $3\frac{1}{8} \times 2\frac{3}{8}$ E.1365–1952

138. Fig Leaf. Design for the title-page to *Leda* by Aldous Huxley, published by Doubleday, Doran & Co. Inc., New York. 1929. (J.P. 615)
Wood-engraving. $1\frac{3}{8} \times 1\frac{1}{4}$ E.1404–1952

139. The Triumph of St. Perpetua. Illustration to *The Passion of Perpetua and Felicity*, translated by Walter Shewring, published as an inset to *The Fleuron*, Number VII by the Cambridge University Press and Doubleday, Doran & Co. Inc., New York, 1930. 1928. (J.P. 555, 1st state)
Wood-engraving. $3\frac{1}{2} \times 3\frac{1}{4}$ E.1360–1952

140. Angel holding a book. Book-plate of Elizabeth Foster and Arthur Carey. 1928. (J.P. 501)
Wood-engraving. $3\frac{5}{8} \times 2\frac{1}{8}$ E.1327–1952

141. Cana of Galilee. Initial letter A used on page 217 of *The Four Gospels*. 1931. (J.P. 814)
Wood-engraving. $2\frac{1}{4} \times 2\frac{1}{8}$ E.1548(2)–1952

142. Trousers and spats. Tail-piece on page 199 of *Clothes* by the artist, 1931. 1930. (J.P. 722)
Wood-engraving. 2×2 E.1491–1952

143. The money bag. Tail-piece to 'The Monk's Tale' on page 165, Volume II of Chaucer's *The Canterbury Tales*, No. 63 of the publications of the Golden Cockerel Press. 1929. (J.P. 602)
Wood-engraving. $2\frac{1}{2} \times 4\frac{1}{2}$ E.1396–1952

144. More's Utopian Alphabet. Illustration on page 138 of *Utopia* by Sir Thomas More, edited by A. W. Reed, No. 65 of the publications of the Golden Cockerel Press. 1929. (J.P. 560)
Wood-engraving. $4\frac{1}{8} \times 2\frac{5}{8}$ E.1367 1952

145. The Roman eagle and SPQR. Initial letter A used on page 203 of *The Four Gospels*, No. 78 of the publications of the Golden Cockerel Press. 1931. (J.P. 808)
Wood-engraving. $2\frac{1}{8} \times 2$ E.1548(1)–1952

146. Ecce tu pulchra es. An illustration, which was not used, to *Canticum Canticorum*, published by the Cranach Press, Weimar, 1931. 1929. (J.P. 614)
Wood-engraving. $5\frac{3}{4} \times 2\frac{3}{4}$ E.1401–1952

147. Nigra sum sed formosa. Frontispiece to *Canticum Canticorum*, published by the Cranach Press, Weimar, 1931. 1929. (J.P. 618)
Wood-engraving. $5\frac{7}{8} \times 2\frac{3}{4}$ E.1408–1952

148. Transiliens colles. Illustration on page 9 of *Canticum Canticorum*, 1931. 1930. (J.P. 666)
Wood-engraving. $5\frac{7}{8} \times 2\frac{3}{4}$ E.1446–1952

149. Sculpture, No. 1. Design, which was not used, for the book-jacket of *Some Modern Sculptors* by Stanley Casson, published by the Oxford University Press. 1930. (J.P. 628)
Wood-engraving. $4\frac{3}{4} \times 2\frac{1}{4}$ E.1417–1952

150. Sculpture, No. 2. Experiment with a multiple tool, 1930. (J.P. 629)
Wood-engraving. $5\frac{1}{8} \times 2\frac{1}{2}$ E.1418–1952

151. Pigotts Roads. A map showing the position of the artist's house Pigotts, North Dean, near Speen, High Wycombe, Buckinghamshire. 1928. (J.P. 556)
Wood-engraving. $4\frac{1}{2} \times 3\frac{1}{8}$ E.1362–1952

152–155. Initial letters for *Canticum Canticorum*. 1931.
Wood-engravings.

    152. Q, with lovers. (J.P. 736) $1 \times 1\frac{1}{8}$
                E.1504(2)–1952
    153. W. (J.P. 744) $\frac{3}{4} \times 1\frac{1}{8}$
                E.1504(10)–1952
    154. I. (J.P. 742) $\frac{3}{4} \times \frac{1}{2}$
                E.1504(8)–1952
    155. M. (J.P. 737) $\frac{3}{4} \times 1$
                E.1504(3)–1952

156. Three alphabets. Illustration on page 65 of *Typography* by the artist, printed by René Hague and Eric Gill, and published by Sheed and Ward Ltd., London. 1931. (J.P. 732, 2nd state)
Wood-engraving. $2\frac{3}{4} \times 3\frac{1}{8}$ E.1501–1952

157. To the King. Dedication in the de luxe edition of *The Testament of Beauty* by Robert Bridges, published by the Clarendon Press, Oxford. 1929. (J.P. 621)
Wood-engraving. $2\frac{3}{8} \times 3$ E.1410–1952

158–163. Decorative borders to Chaucer's *The Canterbury Tales*. 1929, 1930.

    158. Fox on hind legs. Border on page 180, Volume II; pages 32, 58, 130, Volume III; page 105, Volume IV. 1929. (J.P. 573)
    Wood-engraving. $7\frac{3}{8} \times 1\frac{1}{8}$ E.1375(1)–1952
    159. Cock and Hen with three chicks. Border on page 181, Volume II; page 171, Volume III; page 73, Volume IV. 1929. (J.P. 574)
    Wood-engraving. $7\frac{1}{4} \times 1\frac{3}{4}$ E.1375(2)–1952
    160. Naked girl in spray, head thrown back to left, four leaves. Border on pages 2, 68, 120, and 165, Volume III. 1930. (J.P. 646)
    Wood-engraving. $7\frac{1}{4} \times 1\frac{1}{4}$ E.1427(1)–1952

161. Naked girl in spray, head upright, hands over head. Border on pages 69, 181, Volume III; page 80, Volume IV. 1930. (J.P. 647)
Wood-engraving. $7\frac{3}{8} \times 1\frac{3}{4}$ E.1427(2)–1952

162. Death at foot of tree. Border on pages 8, 26, Volume III; pages 74, 116, Volume IV. 1930. (J.P. 632)
Wood-engraving. $7 \times 1\frac{1}{4}$ E.1420(1)–1952

163. Three men hanged. Border on page 27, Volume III. 1930. (J.P. 633)
Wood-engraving. $7\frac{1}{8} \times 1\frac{1}{2}$ E.1420(2)–1952

164. Christ at Emmaus. Illustration embodying the initial word 'And' to St. Luke XXIV, 13 on page 208 of *The Four Gospels*. 1931. (J.P. 810)
Wood-engraving. $2\frac{1}{4} \times 6\frac{1}{4}$ E.1550–1952

165. The Lion of St. Mark. Illustration on page 79 of *The Four Gospels*. 1931. (J.P. 762)
Wood-engraving. $4\frac{1}{2} \times 5\frac{5}{8}$ E.1510–1952

166. The burial of Christ. Illustration embodying the initial word 'And' to St. Luke XXIII, 50 on page 206 of *The Four Gospels*. 1931. (J.P. 809)
Wood-engraving. $7\frac{5}{8} \times 7\frac{1}{2}$ E.1549–1952

167. Design for the cover of the *Journal* of the Royal Institute of British Architects, first used in issue No. 1, Volume 39, Third Series, 7 November 1931. (J.P. 824)
Wood-engraving. $4\frac{1}{2} \times 4\frac{5}{8}$ E.1560–1952

168. Man and woman in a garden. Frontispiece to *The Sonnets of William Shakespeare*, edited by Margaret Flower, printed by René Hague and Eric Gill, and published by Cassell & Co. Ltd., London. 1933. (J.P. 852)
Wood-engraving. $3\frac{3}{4} \times 2\frac{3}{8}$ E.1581–1952

169. Lovers (The Pregnant Wife). 1932. (J.P. 835)
Wood-engraving. $3\frac{3}{8} \times 2\frac{1}{8}$ E.1567–1952

170. 'I am set naked on your kingdom'. Illustration on page 96 of Shakespeare's *Hamlet Prince of Denmark*, 1933. 1932. (J.P. 846)
Wood-engraving. $3\frac{3}{4} \times 3$ E.1575–1952

171. Stag. Book-plate of A. H. Tandy. 1932. (J.P. 839)
Wood-engraving. $3 \times 1\frac{7}{8}$ E.1571–1952

172. Laocoon. Design for the jacket of the *XX Century Library*, published by John Lane Ltd., The Bodley Head, London. 1934. (J.P. 854)
Wood-engraving. $2\frac{7}{8} \times 2\frac{3}{4}$ E.1583–1952

173. The Leisure State. Illustration on page 1 of *Unemployment* by the artist, printed by René Hague and Eric Gill, and published by Faber & Faber Ltd., London. 1933. (J.P. 850)
Wood-engraving. $4\frac{1}{4} \times 3\frac{1}{4}$ E.1579–1952

174. St. John. Illustration on page 47 of *The Passion of Our Lord*, printed by René Hague and Eric Gill, published by Faber & Faber Ltd., London. 1934. (J.P. 865)
Wood-engraving. $5\frac{1}{4} \times 2\frac{3}{8}$ E.1594–1952

175. St. Luke. Illustration on page 33 of *The Passion of Our Lord*. 1934. (J.P. 864)
Wood-engraving. $4\frac{7}{8} \times 2$ E.1593–1952

176. The Single Bed ('Thanks'). Illustration on page 34 of *The Constant Mistress* by Enid Clay, No. 101 of the publications of the Golden Cockerel Press, London. 1934. (J.P. 875)
Wood-engraving. $3 \times 2\frac{3}{4}$ E.1605–1952

177. The Lost Child. Frontispiece to *The Lost Child, and Other Stories* by Mulk Raj Anand, printed by René Hague and Eric Gill, and published by J. A. Allen & Co., London. 1934. (J.P. 855)
Wood-engraving. $5\frac{3}{8} \times 3\frac{3}{8}$ E.1584–1952

178. The Lord's Song. Frontispiece to *The Lord's Song*, a sermon by the artist, No. 91 of the publications of the Golden Cockerel Press. 1934. (J.P. 856)
Wood-engraving. $5\frac{1}{2} \times 2\frac{3}{4}$ E.1585–1952

179. Eve. Book-plate of Jacob Weiss. 1935. (J.P. 885)
Wood-engraving. $3\frac{1}{8} \times 2$ E.1615–1952

180. Clover and monogram DC. Design for the mark of the press of Douglas Cleverdon, the Cloverhill Press. 1935. (J.P. 897)
Wood-engraving. $\frac{7}{8} \times 1$ E.1626–1952

181. History: Man just going on walking. Illustration on the title-pages to the volumes of Shakespeare's historical plays, in the series *The New Temple Shakespeare*, edited by M. R. Ridley, and published by J. M. Dent & Sons Ltd., London and E. P. Dutton & Co. Inc., New York, 1934–1936. 1934. (J.P. 859)
Wood-engraving. $2\frac{5}{8} \times 2\frac{1}{4}$ E.1588–1952

182. Bartimeus. Illustration on the book-jacket of *The Aldine Bible*, edited by M. R. James, O.M., D.LITT., published in 4 volumes by J. M. Dent & Sons Ltd., London. 1934. (J.P. 868)
Wood-engraving. $4 \times 1\frac{7}{8}$ E.1597–1952

183. Title-page to Shakespeare's *Hamlet Prince of Denmark*, printed by René Hague and Eric Gill, for

the Limited Editions Club, New York, 1933. 1932. (J.P. 838)
Wood-engraving. 7¼ × 4½   E.1570–1952

184. Naphill Jubilee Card. 1935. (J.P. 888)
Wood-engraving. 4⅜ × 5½   E.1618–1952

185. Book-plate of Thereze Mary Hope. 1935. (J.P. 883)
Wood-engraving. 2½ × 2⅞   E.1613–1952

186. Apocalypse. Illustration on page 138, Volume IV of *The Aldine Bible*, edited by M. R. James, o.m., d.litt., published by J. M. Dent & Sons Ltd., London. 1936. (J.P. 909)
Wood-engraving. 6¼ × 4¼   E.1638–1952

187. Cherub and ribbon with lettering. Design for the cover of the programme for the evening concert on the third day of the Petersfield Music Festival, 26 April 1935. (J.P. 882)
Wood-engraving. 3⅞ × 3¾   E.1612–1952

188. Woman asleep. Illustration on page 15 of *The Green Ship* by Patrick Miller, No. 111 of the publications of the Golden Cockerel Press. 1936. (J.P. 901)
Wood-engraving. 2¾ × 5   E.1630–1952

189. The fall of Wolsey. Illustration to face page 76 of Shakespeare's *Henry the Eighth*, edited by Herbert Farjeon, published by the Limited Editions Club, New York, 1939. 1937. (J.P. 928)
Wood-engraving. 8⅞ × 5⅞   E.1655–1952

190. Illustration from *Twenty-five nudes*, with an introduction by the artist, printed by René Hague and Eric Gill, and published by J. M. Dent & Sons Ltd., London, 1938. 1937. (J.P. 945)
Wood-engraving. 9⅛ × 5⅝   E.1672–1952

191. Woman looking through foliage. Book-plate of Samuel Kahn. 1936. (J.P. 907)
Wood-engraving. 3⅞ × 3   E.1636–1952

192. Madonna and Child. Design for the Peace Pledge Union, Christmas 1937. (J.P. 932)
Wood-engraving. 5⅞ × 3⅜   E.1659–1952

193. Triton. Design for an end-paper to the volumes in the series *Collins' Illustrated Pocket Classics*, published by William Collins, Sons & Co. Ltd., London, 1936. 1935. (J.P. 890)
Wood-engraving. 4½ × 3   E.1620–1952

194. Eve. Experiment with type-metal. (J.P. 920)
Engraving. 4 × 1½   E.1647–1952

195. Birdhouse. Illustration on the title-page to *Bird House. The Reminiscences of Emma Thurston*

Lamberton, with an introduction by May Lamberton Becker, privately printed for Beatrice Lamberton Warde. 1937. (J.P. 933)
Wood-engraving. 3⅛ × 2   E.1660–1952

196. Rahere. Design which in the 1st state had been used as an illustration on the cover of the *Saint Bartholomew's Hospital Journal*, February and March 1938. 1937. (J.P. 964, 2nd state)
Wood-engraving. 4⅜ × 3¼   E.1691–1952

197. Man and woman embracing. Design to illustrate the card announcing the marriage of Margaret Clay. 1938. (J.P. 979)
Wood-engraving. 2⅝ × 1⅛   E.1706–1952

198. The Pelican and her young. Illustration to *Social Principles & Directions*, second edition, compiled by the artist, published by Hague, Gill and Davey, High Wycombe, Buckinghamshire, 1940. 1939. (J.P. 987)
Wood-engraving. 1⅝ × 2⅝   E.1712–1952

199. David and Goliath. Illustration on page 49 of *The English Bible—Selections*, edited by Arthur Mayhew, published by Ginn & Co. Ltd., London. 1938. (J.P. 982)
Wood-engraving. 3¾ × 3½   E.1708–1952

200. I am a little world. Illustration on page vi of *The Holy Sonnets of John Donne*, with an introduction by Hugh l'A. Fausset, printed by René Hague and Eric Gill, and published by J. M. Dent & Sons Ltd., London. 1938. (J.P. 976)
Woodcut. 5¼ × 3¼   E.1703–1952

201. A Hart. Design for the Ordination Card for Dr. Broomfield, o.s.b. 1939. (J.P. 900)
Wood-engraving. 4¾ × 2½   E.2120–1952

202. Dove with olive branch. Commemorative stamp for the League of Nations Union. 1939. (J.P. 986)
Wood-engraving. 1⅛ × 1⅞   E.2119–1952

203. The Attack. Illustration on the *verso* of the title-page to *The Travels and Sufferings of Father Jean de Brébeuf*, edited and translated by Theodore Besterman, No. 136 of the publications of the Golden Cockerel Press. 1938. (J.P. 972)
Wood-engraving. 4¼ × 5   E.1699–1952

204. Virgin and Child. Christmas Card for the Peace Pledge Union. 1938. (J.P. 980)
Wood-engraving. 5⅛ × 3½   E.2118–1952

205. Blind Girl. Design for an advertisement for the National Institute for the Blind. 1939. (J.P. 991)
Wood-engraving. 5⅝ × 2¼   E.1715–1952

PLATES

1. Chalice and Host with particles. 1914

2. Christmas Card. 1908

3. Self Portrait. 1908

4. Hand and eye. 1908

5. Book-plate. 1909

7. The Slaughter of the Innocents. 1914

6. Funeral Card. 1911

9. Child and Ghost. 1916

10. Decoy Duck. 1915

8. Crucifix. 1913

11. Chalice and Host. 1916

12. St. Michael and the Dragon. 1916

13. Invitation. 1920

14. Flight into Egypt. 1916

15. Woman. 1914

16. Gravestone with Angel. 1916

17. Hog and Wheatsheaf. 1915

18. The Taking of Toll. 1915

19. Animals All. 1916

20. Madonna and Child. 1914

21. The Happy Labourer. 1915

22. D P and Cross. 1916

23. Circular Device. 1916

24. Lettering with nib. 1916

25. Hottentot. 1920

26. The Last Judgment. 1917

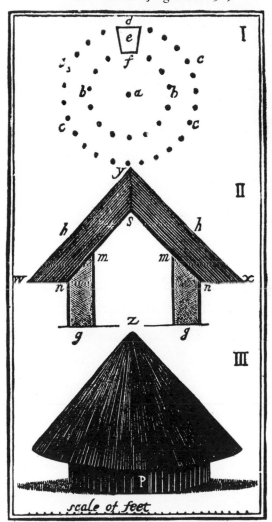

27. Diagram for Ice-House. 1916

19

28. Adam and Eve. 1917

29. Madonna and Child with Chalice. 1916

30. Epiphany. 1917

31. Parlers. 1917

32. Palm Sunday. 1917

33. Jesus dies upon the Cross. 1917

34. Spray of leaves. 1917

35. Paschal Lamb. 1917

36. Initial letter O with speedwell. 1917

37. Welsh Dragon. 1919

39. Crucifix: En Ego. 1918

40. Penny Pie. 1918

38. Flower. 1918

41. Hand and Cross. 1920

42. Tail-piece. 1920

43. Dominican Shield. 1918

44. Stalk with leaves. 1917

21

46. Handscrew; G-cramp; plane. 1917

47. View of Ditchling. 1918

45. Madonna and Child in vesica. 1918

48. Three Martlets. 1914

49. The Holy Face. 1917

50. The Resurrection. 1917

C

51. Christ and the Money-Changers. 1919

52. Spoil Bank Crucifix, with chapel. 1919

53. New England Woods. 1920

54. Penguin. 1920

55. Girl with Deer. 1920

56. Bambino. 1920

57. Lawyer's Wig. 1923

58. St. Martin. 1922

59. The Blessed Trinity with the Blessed Virgin. 1921

60. Tree and Burin. 1921

61. The Lion. 1921

62. Nude Crucifix. 1921

63. Westward Ho! 1921

27

64. Clare. 1922

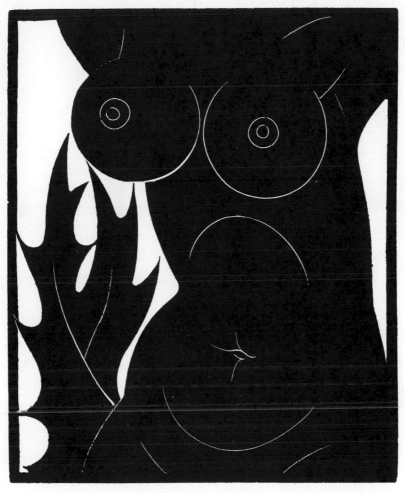

65. The Thorn in the Flesh. 1921

SEDES·SAPIENTIÆ

66. Madonna and Child.
1923

Ex libris THOMAS·MARTIN
FRANCIS·ESMOND·LOWINSKY

67. St. Martin. 1922

68. Nuptials of God. 1922

69. St. George and the Dragon.
1922

70. St. Sebastian. 1922

71. Dress, 1920. 1921

72. Clock Tower. 1922

73. Mary at the Sepulchre. 1923

74. Autumn Midnight. 1923

75. Girl in bath, II. 1923

ORDER *of* INDUSTRIAL HEROISM

INSTITUTED BY
The Daily Herald
Presented as a mark of
respect and admiration
to
a brave man who in a
moment of peril thought
more of others than of
himself

date

76. Daily Herald Order of Industrial Heroism. 1923 (*Reduced*)

77. Jesuit Martyr. 1923

78. Mother and Child. 1924

Gordian G.

79. Gordian Gill. 1924

36

EG

80. Teresa and Winifred Maxwell. 1923

81. Naked Girl lying on Grass. 1924

82. Flower Piece. 1924

83. Death and the Lady. 1924

84

85

86

87

88

84–88. Initial letters for *Autumn Midnight* by Frances Cornford. 1923

89. Woman's Head. 1923

90. Figure of a girl, seated. 1923

91. Crown of Thorns.
1923

92. Sacred Heart with
Crown of Thorns. 1923

93. The Bee Sting. 1924

94. Venus. 1924

95. Youth and Love. 1924

96. The Holy Ghost as Dove. 1923

97. Safety First. 1924

98. The Crucifixion. 1926

99. Adam and Eve in
Heaven, or the
Public-House in
Paradise. 1927

100. Flying Buttresses. 1926

101. The Shepherds. 1924

RALPH EDWARD
GATHORNE·HARDY

102. Book-plate. 1925

103. Girl with Three Scallops. 1927

104. Roundel, with a crouching figure
by Aristide Maillol. 1925

105. Earth Waiting. 1926

45

106. Crucifix. 1926

107. St. Thomas's Hands. 1926

108. Boy with drawing-board. 1925

46

109. St. Bernadette. 1926

110. A Garden enclosed. 1925

111. Tail-piece. 1927

112. Eve. 1926

113. The Good Shepherd. 1927

115. The Convert. 1925

114. Design for book-plate. 1925

116. Girl in leaves. 1926

117. Woman Bending. 1926

118. Dalliance. 1926

119. On my Bed by Night. 1925

50

120. The Bird in the Bush. 1928

121. The Skaters. 1926

122–124. Borders to pages in Chaucer's *Troilus and Criseyde*, published by the Golden Cockerel Press. 1927

125   126   127

125–127. Borders to pages in Chaucer's *Troilus and Criseyde*, published by the Golden Cockerel Press. 1927

T

SAPON

BMW

LTN

128. Letters for Chaucer's *Troilus and Criseyde*, published by the Golden Cockerel Press. 1927

ABC
DEFGHIK
LMNOPR
STUVW
XYZ
JQ

129. Letters for the Golden Cockerel Press. 1928

130. Approaching Dawn. 1927

GLORIA·IN·PROFUNDIS

131. Nativity. 1927

132. Marbling. 1929

133. Leda loved. 1929

134. Venus and Cupid with the Golden Cockerel. 1928

135. The Parson's Tale. 1930

136. Amnon. 1930

137. Belle Sauvage I. 1929

138. Fig Leaf. 1929

139. The Triumph of St. Perpetua. 1928

140. Angel holding a book. 1928

141. Cana of Galilee. 1931

142. Trousers and spats. 1930

143. The money bag. 1929

144. More's Utopian Alphabet. 1929

145. The Roman eagle and SPQR.
1931

146. Ecce tu pulchra es. 1929

147. Nigra sum sed formosa. 1929

148. Transiliens colles. 1930

66

149. Sculpture, No. 1. 1930

150. Sculpture, No. 2. 1930

67

151. Pigotts Roads. 1928

152 153 154 155

152–155. Initial letters for the Cranach Press *Canticum Canticorum*. 1931.

156. Three alphabets. 1931

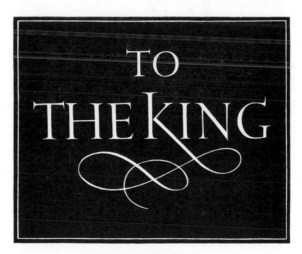

157. To the King. 1929

158   159   160

158–160. Borders to pages in Chaucer's *The Canterbury Tales*, published by
the Golden Cockerel Press. 1929 & 1930

161 162 163

161–163. Borders to pages in Chaucer's *The Canterbury Tales*, published by
the Golden Cockerel Press. 1929 & 1930

164. Christ at Emmaus. 1931

165. The Lion of St. Mark. 1931

166. The Burial of Christ. 1931

167. Cover design for the *Journal* of the Royal Institute of British Architects. 1931

168. Man and woman in a garden. 1933

169. Lovers (The Pregnant Wife).
1932

170. 'I am set naked on your kingdom.' 1932

171. Stag. 1932

172. Laocoon. 1934

173. The Leisure State. 1933

174. St. John. 1934

175. St. Luke. 1934

176. The Single Bed ('Thanks'). 1934

77

177. The Lost Child. 1934

178. The Lord's Song. 1934

78

EX LI-BRIS JACOB WEISS

179. Eve. 1935

180. Design for
Douglas Cleverdon.
1935

181. History. 1934

182. Bartimeus. 1934

G

183. Title-page to Shakespeare's *Hamlet*, published by the
Limited Editions Club, New York, 1933.

184. Naphill Jubilee Card. 1935

185. Book-plate. 1935

186. Apocalypse. 1936

187. Cherub and ribbon with lettering. 1935

188. Woman asleep. 1936

189. The fall of Wolsey. 1937

190. Female nude. 1937

Ex Libris
SAMUEL
KAHN

191. Woman looking through foliage. 1936

192. Madonna and Child. 1937

194. Eve. 1936

193. Triton. 1935

195. Birdhouse. 1937

196 Rahere. 1937

197. Man and woman embracing. 1938

198. The Pelican and her young. 1939

199. David and Goliath. 1938

200. I am a little world. 1938

As the   hart de-
sireth   the water
brooks;   so

long-   eth my
soul   after thee,
O God.

201. A Hart. 1939

202. Dove with olive
branch. 1939

91

203. The Attack. 1938

204. Christmas Card. 1938

205. Blind Girl. 1939